frame>by>frame
asian

frame>by>frame
asian
a visual step-by-step cookbook

LOVE
FOOD™

First published in 2010
LOVE FOOD is an imprint of Parragon Books Ltd

Parragon
Queen Street House
4 Queen Street
Bath BA1 1HE, UK

ISBN: 978-1-4075-5334-4

Printed in China

Designed by Talking Design
Photography by Mike Cooper
Home economy by Lincoln Jefferson
New recipes by Christine France
Introduction by Linda Doeser

Notes for the Reader
This book uses both metric and imperial measurements. Follow the same units of measurement throughout; do not mix metric and imperial. All spoon measurements are level: teaspoons are assumed to be 5 ml, and tablespoons are assumed to be 15 ml. Unless otherwise stated, milk is assumed to be full fat, eggs and individual vegetables are medium, and pepper is freshly ground black pepper.

The times given are an approximate guide only. Preparation times differ according to the techniques used by different people and the cooking times may also vary from those given. Optional ingredients, variations or serving suggestions have not been included in the calculations.

Recipes using raw or very lightly cooked eggs, fish, meat or poultry should be avoided by infants, the elderly, pregnant women, convalescents and anyone suffering from an illness. Pregnant and breastfeeding women are advised to avoid eating peanuts and peanut products. Sufferers from nut allergies should be aware that some of the ready-made ingredients used in the recipes in this book may contain nuts. Always check the packaging before use.

Although sushi is traditionally made using both raw and cooked fish, all of the sushi recipes in this book can be made with cooked fish. If you are using raw fish, then ensure that it is as fresh as possible, has been bought from a reputable supplier selling sushi- or sashimi-grade fish and has been stored at a low temperature in a refrigerator until serving. Ensure that fish is prepared using clean utensils.

contents

introduction

This superlative cookbook with its wealth of lovely and tremendously useful photographs will prove to be an invaluable and delightful addition to any cook's bookshelf. The recipes are clear, easy to follow, beautifully illustrated, wonderfully tasty and truly authentic, so whatever your level of expertise in the kitchen you are virtually guaranteed success every time.

Every recipe starts with a photograph of all the ingredients but this is more than just a pretty picture or – even less helpful – a montage that is not to scale so that a crab claw appears to be the same size as a duck. Instead, it serves as a handy way of checking that you have everything ready before you start cooking. Just comparing the picture with the ingredients arranged on your own worktop or kitchen table will ensure that you haven't missed anything out and when it's time to add the coriander, for example, you have already chopped it as specified in the ingredients list. If you're uncertain about how thinly to slice lemon grass or how finely to dice prawns, a glance at the photograph will provide an instant answer.

Each short and straightforward step of the method is clearly explained without any jargon or difficult technical terms. Once again, what you see in the photograph is what you should expect to see in front of you. Not only is this reassuring for the novice cook, but those with more experience will also find it a helpful reminder of the little touches that can easily be overlooked. Each recipe ends with a mouth-watering photograph of the finished dish, complete with any serving suggestions.

Why you need this book

Asian food, whether Chinese, Thai, Japanese, Indonesian or Malaysian, has been popular in the West for decades and Western cooks have become increasingly adventurous about trying out recipes in their own kitchens, particularly since speciality ingredients have now become widely available. Asian food is designed as much to please the eye as it is to please the palate and while many dishes, especially stir-fries, can be cooked in minutes, they are all prepared with attention to detail and an impressive balance of complementary flavours. The 60 easy-to follow recipes in this book will enable you to re-create the authentic taste, texture and appearance of Asia without leaving home.

You can simply pick and mix individual dishes for a midweek family supper or create a formal 'banquet' for a special occasion with soup, wraps, stir-fries, curries, roasts and, of course, rice and noodles, all arranged on the table together, followed by exotic ice cream or sticky fried fruit.

> 1 > 2 > 3

top tips for success

> Read all the way through the recipe – ingredients list and method – before you start so that you will know exactly what you will need. Scrabbling about at the back of the storecupboard to find a rarely used ingredient or moving half a dozen other utensils to reach the one you require in the middle of cooking a dish is, at best, exasperating and, at worst, liable to result in a scorched stir-fry or boiling over rice.

> Do try to obtain any more unusual ingredients, such as galangal and Chinese chives – perhaps from a Chinese supermarket, which will often stock ingredients from many other Asian countries – to create a truly authentic flavour and unique aroma.

> Note that there is a difference between coconut milk, widely available in cans and extensively used in Thai and Indonesian cuisine, and the thin almost colourless liquid found inside a fresh coconut. The canned milk is made by steeping shredded coconut flesh in water and is a thicker, creamy liquid.

> Always cut beef across the grain, otherwise it becomes tough. Lamb, pork and poultry may be cut along or across the grain.

> If you need to cut meat into paper-thin slices, put it in the freezer for about 1 hour beforehand to firm up.

> A new wok should always be seasoned before it is used, unless it has a non-stick lining. This process seals the surface. First, scrub the wok with cream cleanser to remove the manufacturer's protective coating of oil. Put the wok over a low heat and add 2 tablespoons vegetable oil. Make a pad of kitchen paper and wipe the oil all over the inside of the wok, then heat gently for about 10 minutes. Remove from the heat and wipe off the oil with more pads of kitchen paper, all of which will become black. Reheat the wok with another 2 tablespoons oil, spreading it over the surface with a pad of kitchen paper. Heat for a further 10 minutes, then wipe out with pads of kitchen paper as before. Continue repeating this process until the pads of kitchen paper no longer turn black. The wok is now ready for use. (For further information see page 11.)

> Spring roll wrappers: There are two types. Those made from rice flour must be soaked in water before using to make them flexible. Wheat flour wrappers are usually sold frozen. Leave them to thaw at room temperature for a couple of hours, then separate gently.

> Remember that Japanese soy sauce, sometimes simply called shoyu but also known as usukuchi (light) and tamari (regular), is nothing like as strongly flavoured as Chinese.

time - saving shortcuts

> To peel garlic, lightly crush a clove with the flat blade of a cook's knife or cleaver. Then the skin is easy to remove.

> To prepare fresh ginger, peel off the skin with a paring knife. Put the ginger on a chopping board and lightly crush with the flat blade of a cook's knife or cleaver, then chop or cut into shreds.

> To prepare chillies, slice them lengthways and scrape out the seeds and membranes with the tip of the knife. The heat of chillies is in the membranes rather than the seeds, but removing the seeds tends to scrape out the membranes at the same time. If you like really fiery dishes, don't bother.

> To prepare lemon grass, cut off the dry tops to leave about 15 cm/6 inches stalk. Peel off any coarse outer layers. Put the lemon grass on a chopping board, put the flat side of a cook's knife or a cleaver on top and hit it with your fist to bruise, then cut into thin slices. Finally, chop finely. You can also use lemon grass without chopping but, if you do, it must be removed and discarded before the dish is served.

> Use kitchen scissors to snip fresh herbs rather than chopping with a knife.

useful equipment

> **Wok:** This is probably the only essential piece of specialist equipment that isn't standard in a Western kitchen. It is a large, bowl-shaped pan – ideally about 35 cm/14 inches in diameter – with deep sloping sides and a round or flat base. Use the former with a metal stand on a gas hob and the latter on an electric one. It is primarily used for stir-frying, but is also useful for steaming, deep-frying and braising. The best woks are made of carbon steel, which can withstand the high temperature required for stir-frying; stainless steel woks tend to scorch and non-stick woks must be used at lower than ideal temperatures. A wok with handles on either side is easy to lift. Others may have a single long handle or one long handle and one smaller,

ear-shaped handle opposite. A new wok must be seasoned before use (see page 10). If the wok is not supplied with a lid, it is worth buying a large, domed cover for steaming. It is possible to stir-fry in a large frying pan but it is more difficult. The shape of the wok makes it very easy to toss the ingredients from the centre to the sides without throwing them all over the hob. To stir-fry in a wok, preheat it thoroughly before adding any oil, which should then be swirled so that it covers the base and comes halfway up the sides. Start cooking with aromatics, then the ingredients that need the longest cooking time and, finally, gradually add the rest.

> **Steamer:** A Western-style steamer may be used to cook Asian dishes, but it is worth considering buying bamboo steamers. They are inexpensive, designed to stack and rest on the sloping sides of a wok just above the water level. They are available in a range of sizes and may also be used for serving. If you are planning to steam an ingredient, such as fish fillets, on a plate, you will require a trivet that can stand on the base of the wok and keep the plate above the water level.

> **Knives:** Good-quality, heavy and well-balanced knives are essential in any kitchen. The minimum requirements are a paring, vegetable, utility and cook's knife. Keep them sharpened using a V-sharpener, carborundum stone or steel and store them in a knife block. Sharp knives are not only easier to use, but are also safer as they are less liable to slip. Consider buying a cleaver. Most Western cooks find these heavy cutting tools somewhat unwieldy to begin with but it is worth persevering as they serve many purposes from general chopping – including slicing effortlessly through ribs – to delicate tasks such as deveining prawns.

> **Chopping boards:** Wooden boards are inexpensive, have natural anti-bacterial properties, are gentle with knife blades and are easy to wash or scrub in hot soapy water. Their disadvantages are that they are often heavy and bulky, so may cause storage problems, and they cannot be sterilized. Plastic boards have a rough texture to prevent slipping, are thinner and lighter, can be washed in the dishwasher and sterilized. They usually come in a range of colours so it is easy to make sure that you use different boards for raw meat, poultry and vegetables.

> **Wok accessories:** None of these is essential as you can use utensils easily found in any kitchen. However, they add to the authenticity and you may find them helpful. A wok scoop consists of a wide metal mesh basket on the end of a long wooden handle. It makes stir-frying easy, but you could use a long-handled spoon. A wok brush consists of a bundle of split bamboo used for cleaning your wok. You can simply use a washing-up brush.

> **Cook's chopsticks:** These extra-long chopsticks can be used for adding ingredients, stirring, separating noodles and fluffing up rice. Of course, you can use a spoon and a fork but it's quite fun to use authentic implements and they are much easier to manipulate than they seem at first sight. To use chopsticks, place one in the curve between your forefinger and thumb. Pick up the second stick like a pencil. Keep the first stick still for stability and manipulate the second stick to pick up pieces of meat and vegetables.

starters & soups

>4

>5

>6

thai tom yum soup with fish

serves 6

ingredients

1.5 litres/2¾ pints light chicken stock

6 lemon grass stalks, crushed to release their flavour

3 tbsp very finely chopped coriander roots

10 kaffir lime leaves, central stalks torn off

1 red chilli, deseeded and finely chopped

2.5-cm/1-inch piece of galangal (or fresh ginger), peeled and thinly sliced

3 tbsp fish sauce, plus extra, to taste

1 tbsp sugar, plus extra, to taste

500 g/1 lb 2 oz raw prawns, peeled and deveined

500 g/1 lb 2 oz firm white fish, such as cod or monkfish, chopped into bite-sized pieces

225 g/8 oz canned bamboo shoots or water chestnuts

12 cherry tomatoes, halved

juice of 2 limes

handful fresh coriander leaves and handful fresh basil leaves, chopped, to garnish

> **1** Pour the stock into a large saucepan.

> **2** Add the lemon grass, coriander roots, kaffir lime leaves, chilli, galangal, fish sauce and sugar. Cover the saucepan.

> **3** Bring to the boil, then reduce the heat and simmer for 10 minutes.

> **4** Add the prawns, fish and bamboo shoots and simmer for a further 4 minutes.

>5 Add the tomatoes and lime juice and check the seasoning, adding more fish sauce and sugar, if necessary.

>6 Remove and discard the lemon grass stalks, then divide the soup between six bowls.

Scatter over the coriander
and basil leaves and serve.

hot & sour soup tom yum

serves 4

ingredients

2 fresh red chillies, deseeded and roughly chopped

6 tbsp rice vinegar

1.2 litres/2 pints vegetable stock

2 lemon grass stalks, halved

4 tbsp soy sauce

1 tbsp palm sugar

juice of ½ lime

2 tbsp groundnut or vegetable oil

225 g/8 oz firm tofu (drained weight), cut into 1-cm/½-inch cubes

400 g/14 oz canned straw mushrooms, drained

4 spring onions, chopped

1 small head pak choi, shredded

> **1** Mix the chillies and vinegar together in a non-reactive bowl, cover and leave to stand at room temperature for 1 hour.

> **2** Meanwhile, bring the stock to the boil in a saucepan. Add the lemon grass, soy sauce, sugar and lime juice, reduce the heat and simmer for 20–30 minutes.

> **3** Heat the oil in a preheated wok, add the tofu cubes and stir-fry over a high heat for 2–3 minutes, or until browned all over. (You may need to do this in 2 batches, depending on the size of the wok.)

> **4** Remove with a slotted spoon and drain on kitchen paper.

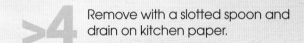

21

>5 Add the chillies and vinegar with the tofu, mushrooms and half the spring onions to the stock mixture and cook for 10 minutes.

 >6 Mix the remaining spring onions with the pak choi.

Scatter over the spring onions and pak
choi and serve.

miso soup

serves 4

ingredients
1 litre/1¾ pints water
2 tsp dashi granules
175 g/6 oz silken tofu, drained
   and cut into small cubes
4 shiitake mushrooms or white
   mushrooms, finely sliced
4 tbsp miso paste
2 spring onions, chopped

>1 Put the water in a large pan with the dashi granules and bring to a boil.

>2 Add the tofu and mushrooms, reduce the heat, and let simmer for 3 minutes.

The miso paste will begin to settle, so stir the soup before serving to recombine.

>3 Stir in the miso paste and let simmer gently, stirring, until it has dissolved.

>4 Add the spring onions and serve immediately.

thai salmon laksa

serves 4

ingredients

juice and zest of 2 limes
2 tbsp sunflower oil
1 red chilli, deseeded and finely
   chopped
4 garlic cloves, peeled and
   crushed

2.5-cm/1-inch piece fresh
   ginger, peeled and grated
1 tsp ground coriander
small bunch of fresh coriander,
   plus extra to garnish
3 tbsp nam pla
500 ml/18 fl oz vegetable or fish
   stock

850 ml/1½ pints canned
   coconut milk
3 carrots, peeled and very
   thinly sliced
400 g/14 oz noodles
1 tbsp sesame oil
1 tbsp vegetable oil
200 g/7 oz broccoli florets

500 g/1 lb 2 oz salmon fillet,
   skinned, boned and cut into
   slices half the width of a finger

2 Place a large saucepan over a medium heat and add the paste. Fry for 1 minute.

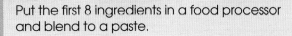 **1** Put the first 8 ingredients in a food processor and blend to a paste.

3 Add the stock, coconut milk and carrots and bring to the boil. Simmer whilst you cook the noodles according to the packet instructions.

4 Drain the noodles and return to the warm saucepan with a splash of sesame oil and vegetable oil. Cover.

>5 Add the broccoli to the liquid, bring back to the boil and then turn off the heat and add the salmon slices, gently stirring them in. Leave to stand for 3 minutes.

>6 Place a handful of noodles in each bowl, then ladle in the laksa.

Sprinkle with coriander
leaves and serve.

chicken noodle soup

serves 4–6

ingredients

2 skinless chicken breasts
2 litres/3½ pints water
1 onion, with skin left on,
  cut in half
1 large garlic clove, cut in half

1-cm/½-inch piece fresh ginger,
  peeled and sliced
4 black peppercorns, lightly
  crushed
4 cloves
2 star anise

1 celery stick, chopped
100 g/3½ oz baby corn cobs,
  sliced
2 spring onions, finely shredded
115 g/4 oz dried rice vermicelli
  noodles

1 carrot, peeled and coarsely
  grated
salt and pepper

> **1** Put the chicken breasts and water into a saucepan and bring to the boil. Reduce the heat and simmer, skimming the surface until no more foam rises.

> **2** Add the onion, garlic, ginger, peppercorns, cloves, star anise and a pinch of salt.

> **3** Continue to simmer for 20 minutes, or until the chicken is tender and cooked through.

> **4** Remove the chicken and set aside about 1.2 litres/2 pints of stock. Add the celery, baby corn cobs and spring onions.

5 Bring the stock to the boil and boil until the baby corn cobs are almost tender, then add the noodles and continue boiling for 2 minutes.

6 Meanwhile, chop the chicken, add to the pan with the grated carrot and continue cooking for about 1 minute, until the chicken is re-heated and the noodles are soft. Add seasoning to taste.

Transfer to bowls and serve.

hoisin & sesame-glazed grilled duck

serves 4

ingredients

2 duck breasts,
  about 225 g/8 oz each
½ tsp ground star anise
3 tbsp hoisin sauce
1 tbsp sesame oil
1 ripe mango
½ cucumber
4 spring onions
1 tbsp rice vinegar
toasted sesame seeds,
  to sprinkle

> **>1** Using a sharp knife, score the skin of the duck breast in a diamond pattern.

> **>2** Mix the star anise, hoisin sauce and sesame oil and brush over the duck. Cover and marinate for at least 30 minutes.

Serve the duck slices arranged over a spoonful of the mango salad, sprinkled with sesame seeds.

>3 Peel, stone and thinly slice the mango. Cut the cucumber into matchsticks and thinly slice the onions. Stir together and sprinkle with vinegar.

>4 Preheat the grill to hot. Grill the duck for 8–10 minutes on each side, brushing with the marinade. Rest for 5 minutes, then slice thinly.

tempura vegetables

serves 4

ingredients
150 g/5½ oz packet
   tempura mix
4 shiitake mushrooms
4 fresh asparagus spears
4 slices sweet potato

1 red pepper, deseeded and
   cut into strips
4 onion slices, cut widthwise
   into rings
oil, for deep-frying

dipping sauce
2 tsp mirin
1 tbsp shoyu
   (Japanese soy sauce)

pinch of dashi granules,
   dissolved in 2 tbsp
   boiling water

>1 To make the dipping sauce, mix the ingredients together in a small dipping dish.

>2 Mix the tempura with water according to the packet instructions.

>3 Drop the vegetables into the batter.

>4 Heat enough oil for deep-frying in a wok, deep-fat fryer or large heavy-based saucepan until it reaches 180–190°C/ 350–375°F, or until a cube of bread browns in 30 seconds. Fry the toasts prawn-side down for about 2 minutes. Turn and fry for a further 2 minutes until golden.

37

>5 Lift 2–3 pieces of the vegetables out of the batter, add to the oil, and cook for 2–3 minutes, or until the batter is a light golden colour.

>6 Remove the tempura vegetables with a slotted spoon and drain on kitchen paper. Keep hot while you cook the remaining pieces.

Transfer the tempura vegetables to a serving dish and serve with the dipping sauce.

pork & cabbage gyoza

makes 24

ingredients
24 gyoza wonton skins
2 tbsp water, for brushing
oil, for pan-frying
2 tbsp Japanese rice vinegar
2 tbsp shoyu (Japanese
  soy sauce)

filling
100 g/3½ oz Napa cabbage,
  finely shredded
2 spring onions, finely chopped
115 g/4 oz fresh pork mince
1-cm/½-inch piece fresh ginger,
  finely grated

2 garlic cloves, crushed
1 tbsp shoyu (Japanese
  soy sauce)
2 tsp mirin
pinch of white pepper
salt, to taste

40

To make the filling, mix all the ingredients together in a bowl.

Lay a gyoza wonton skin in the palm of your hand and place 1 heaped teaspoon of the filling in the centre. Brush a little water around the edges of the wonton skin.

>3 Fold the skin sides up to meet in a ridge along the centre and press the edges together. Brush the curved edges of the skin with a little more water and make a series of little folds along the edges.

>4 Repeat with the remaining gyoza wonton wrappers and filling. Heat a little oil in a deep lidded frying pan and add as many gyoza as will fill the bottom of the pan with just a little space in between.

>5 Cook for 2 minutes, or until browned. Add water to a depth of 3 mm/⅛ inch, cover the pan, and let simmer over a low heat for 6 minutes, or until the wrappers are translucent and cooked. Remove and keep warm while you cook the remaining gyoza.

>6 Put the vinegar in a small dipping dish, stir in the shoyu, and add a splash of water.

Transfer the gyoza to a serving
dish and serve with the sauce
for dipping.

prawn toasts

makes 16 pieces

ingredients

100 g/3½ oz raw prawns,
  peeled and deveined
2 egg whites
2 tbsp cornflour
½ tsp sugar
pinch of salt
2 tbsp finely chopped fresh
  coriander leaves
2 slices day-old white bread
vegetable or groundnut oil, for
  deep-frying

>1 Pound the prawns to a pulp with a pestle and mortar.

>2 Mix the prawns with one of the egg whites and 1 tablespoon of the cornflour. Add the sugar and salt and stir in the coriander. Mix the remaining egg white with the remaining cornflour.

Remove the prawn toasts with a slotted spoon, drain on kitchen paper and serve warm.

>3 Remove the crusts from the bread and cut each slice into 8 triangles. Brush the top of each piece with the egg white and cornflour mixture, then add 1 teaspoon of the prawn mixture. Smooth the top.

>4 Heat enough oil for deep-frying in a wok, deep-fat fryer or large heavy-based saucepan until it reaches 180–190°C/350–375°F, or until a cube of bread browns in 30 seconds. Fry the toasts prawn-side down for about 2 minutes. Turn and fry for a further 2 minutes until golden.

45

chicken satay skewers with peanut sauce

serves 4

ingredients
4 skinless, boneless chicken
   breasts, about 115 g/4 oz
   each, cut into 2-cm/¾-inch
   cubes
4 tbsp soy sauce
1 tbsp cornflour
2 garlic cloves, finely chopped

2.5-cm/1-inch piece fresh
   ginger, peeled and finely
   chopped
cucumber, roughly chopped,
   to serve

peanut sauce
2 tbsp groundnut or
   vegetable oil
½ onion, finely chopped
1 garlic clove, finely chopped
4 tbsp crunchy peanut butter
4–5 tbsp water
½ tsp chilli powder

> 1 Put the chicken cubes in a shallow dish.

> 2 Mix the soy sauce, cornflour, garlic and ginger together in a small bowl and pour over the chicken. Cover and leave to marinate in the refrigerator for at least 2 hours.

> 3 Meanwhile, soak 12 bamboo skewers in cold water for at least 30 minutes.

> 4 Preheat the oven. Thread the chicken pieces onto the bamboo skewers.

>5 Transfer the skewers to a griddle pan and cook under a preheated grill for 3–4 minutes.

>6 Turn the skewers over and cook for a further 3–4 minutes or until cooked through.

>7 Meanwhile, to make the sauce, heat the oil in a saucepan, add the onion and garlic and cook over a medium heat, stirring frequently, for 3–4 minutes until softened.

>8 Add the peanut butter, water and chilli powder and simmer for 2–3 minutes until softened and thinned.

Serve the skewers immediately with the warm sauce and cucumber.

crab wontons

serves 4

ingredients

1 tbsp groundnut or vegetable oil, plus extra for deep-frying
2.5-cm/1-inch piece fresh ginger, peeled and finely chopped

¼ red pepper, deseeded and finely chopped
handful of fresh coriander, chopped
¼ tsp salt

150 g/5½ oz canned white crabmeat, drained
20 wonton wrappers
water, for brushing
sweet chilli dipping sauce, to serve

> **1** Heat the oil in a preheated wok.

> **2** Add the ginger and red pepper and stir-fry over a high heat for 30 seconds.

> **3** Add the coriander and mix well. Leave to cool, then add the salt and the crabmeat and mix well. Meanwhile remove the wrappers from the packet, but keep in a pile covered with clingfilm to prevent them from drying out.

> **4** Lay one wrapper on a work surface in front of you and brush the edges with water. Put a teaspoonful of the crabmeat mixture in the centre and fold the wrapper over the mixture to form a triangle.

> **5** Press the edges together to seal. Fold each side corner up to the top corner to make a small parcel, brushing the edges with water to seal if necessary. Repeat with the remaining wrappers and crabmeat mixture.

> **6** Heat the oil for deep-frying in the wok or a deep saucepan or deep-fat fryer to 180–190°C/350–375°F, or until a cube of bread browns in 30 seconds.

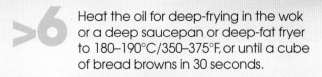

> **7** Add the wontons, in batches, and cook for 45 seconds–1 minute until crisp and golden all over.

> **8** Remove with a slotted spoon, drain on kitchen paper and keep warm while you cook the remaining wontons.

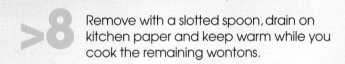

Serve with sweet chilli dipping sauce.

vietnamese-style vegetable wraps

serves 4

ingredients

2 medium carrots
2 sticks celery
1 tbsp rice vinegar
½ tsp salt
2 spring onions
115 g/4 oz beansprouts
small handful coriander leaves,
    chopped
small handful mint leaves,
    chopped
small handful basil leaves,
    chopped
8 Little Gem lettuce leaves

dressing

2 garlic cloves,
    chopped
1 red chilli, deseeded
    and chopped
1 tbsp palm sugar
2 tbsp lime juice
2 tbsp fish sauce

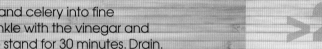

>1 Slice the carrots and celery into fine matchsticks. Sprinkle with the vinegar and salt and leave to stand for 30 minutes. Drain.

>2 Thinly slice the spring onions and mix with the carrots, celery, beansprouts and herbs.

Transfer the wraps to a serving dish and serve with the remaining dressing.

>3 To make the dressing, mash the garlic, chilli and palm sugar in a pestle and mortar, then stir in the lime juice, fish sauce and 2 tbsp water.

>4 Divide the vegetables between the lettuce leaves and spoon 1 teaspoon of the dressing over each leaf.

spring rolls

makes 20–25 pieces

ingredients

6 dried Chinese mushrooms,
  soaked in warm water for
  20 minutes
1 tbsp vegetable or groundnut
  oil, plus extra for deep-frying
225 g/8 oz minced pork

1 tsp dark soy sauce
100 g/3½ oz canned bamboo
  shoots, rinsed and julienned
pinch of salt
100 g/3½ oz raw prawns,
  peeled, deveined and
  chopped

225 g/8 oz beansprouts,
  trimmed and roughly
  chopped
1 tbsp spring onions,
  finely chopped
20–25 spring roll wrappers
1 egg white, lightly beaten

> **1** Squeeze out any excess water from the mushrooms and finely slice, discarding any tough stems.

> **2** In a preheated wok or deep pan, heat the oil and stir-fry the pork until it changes colour.

> **3** Add the dark soy sauce, bamboo shoots, mushrooms and a little salt. Stir over a high heat for 3 minutes.

> **4** Add the prawns and cook for 2 minutes, then add the beansprouts and cook for a further minute. Remove from the heat and stir in the spring onions. Leave to cool.

> **5** Place a tablespoon of the mixture towards the bottom of a wrapper. Roll once to secure the filling, then fold in the sides to create a 10-cm/4-inch piece and continue to roll up. Seal with egg white.

> **6** Heat enough oil for deep-frying in a wok, deep-fat fryer or large heavy-based saucepan until it reaches 180–190°C/350–375°F, or until a cube of bread browns in 30 seconds. Fry the rolls for about 5 minutes, until golden brown and crispy.

Transfer the spring rolls to serving
bowls and serve.

sashimi

serves 2

ingredients
1 fresh mackerel, cleaned and
   filleted
90 ml/3 fl oz rice vinegar
3 raw scallops, in their shells
150 g/5½ oz fresh (sushi-grade)
   tuna (maguro)
150 g/5½ oz fresh (sushi-grade)
   salmon (sake)

to garnish
chopped daikon
fresh chives
sliced ginger
wasabi paste
shoyu (Japanese soy sauce),
   to serve

> **1** Put the mackerel fillets and rice vinegar in a shallow, nonmetallic dish, cover with clingfilm, and let marinate in the refrigerator for 1 hour.

> **2** Remove the mackerel from the marinade and pat dry with kitchen paper. Skin, then slice the flesh diagonally.

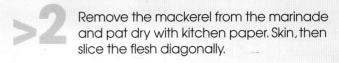

> **3** Remove the scallops from their shells. Separate any corals from the bodies, remove and discard the white frills and any black matter and also the membrane around the edge of the scallops. Slice each scallop horizontally in half.

> **4** Put the scallops in a heatproof dish and pour over boiling water to cover. Using a slotted spoon, remove immediately and pat dry with kitchen paper.

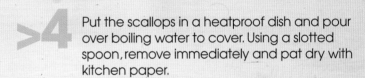

>5 Shape the tuna and salmon into neat rectangles, then slice into smaller rectangular slices.

>6 Arrange all the fish on a serving platter with the chopped daikon.

Garnish with fresh chives and serve with the
sliced ginger, wasabi paste and shoyu.

sticky ginger & soy chicken wings

serves 4

ingredients

12 chicken wings
2 garlic cloves, crushed
2.5-cm/1-inch piece fresh
  ginger
2 tbsp dark soy sauce

2 tbsp lime juice
1 tbsp clear honey
1 tsp chilli sauce
2 tsp sesame oil
lime wedges, to serve

>1 Tuck the pointed tip of each wing under the thicker end to make a neat triangle.

>2 Mix together the garlic, ginger, soy sauce, lime, honey, chilli sauce and oil.

Serve hot, with lime wedges.

>3 Spoon the mixture over the chicken and turn to coat evenly. Cover and marinate for several hours or overnight.

>4 Preheat the grill to hot. Cook the wings on a foil-lined grill pan for 12–15 minutes, or until the juices have no trace of pink when pierced, basting often with the marinade.

noodles & rice

>4

>5

>6

scattered sushi & smoked mackerel

makes 24

ingredients
8 mangetout
5-cm/2-inch piece daikon
finely grated rind and juice of
   lemon
2 spring onions, finely chopped

2 smoked mackerel, skinned
   and cut into diagonal strips
½ cucumber, peeled and cut
   into slices
salt

garnish
pickled ginger
strips of toasted nori
wasabi paste

sushi rice
215 g/7¼ oz short-grain rice
350 ml/12 fl oz water

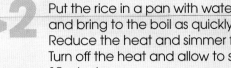

>1 Put the rice in a strainer and rinse in cold water until the water is clear, then drain.

>2 Put the rice in a pan with water, cover and bring to the boil as quickly as possible. Reduce the heat and simmer for 10 minutes. Turn off the heat and allow to stand for 15 minutes.

>3 Transfer the rice to a bowl and add the salt.

>4 Cook the mangetout in a pan of boiling salted water for 1 minute. Drain and cool.

>5 Using a sharp knife, shred the daikon into long, thin slices and cut each slice lengthways as finely as you can.

>6 Mix the rice with the lemon rind and juice.

>7 Divide the cooked rice between four bowls and sprinkle the spring onions over the top.

>8 Arrange the mackerel, cucumber, mangetout and daikon on top of the rice.

Garnish with pickled ginger, nori strips and wasabi paste and serve.

udon noodle stir-fry with fish cakes & ginger

serves 2

ingredients

2 x 150-g/5½-oz packs
  ready-to-wok udon noodles
1 leek, shredded
200 g/7 oz beansprouts
8 shiitake mushrooms, finely
  sliced

2 pieces Japanese fish cake,
  sliced
12 raw prawns, peeled and
  deveined
2 eggs, beaten
oil, for stir-frying

2 tbsp shoyu (Japanese
  soy sauce)
3 tbsp mirin
2 tbsp chopped fresh
  coriander leaves

to serve

chilli oil
2 spring onions, finely sliced
2 tbsp shredded beni-shoga
  (red ginger)

1 Rinse the noodles under cold running water to remove any oil and tip into a bowl.

2 Add the leek, bean sprouts, mushrooms, fish cake, prawns and eggs to the noodles and mix well to combine.

3 Preheat a wok over high heat. Add a little oil and heat until very hot.

4 Add the noodle mixture and stir-fry until golden, and the prawns have turned pink and are cooked through.

>5 Add the shoyu, mirin and coriander and toss together.

>6 Divide the noodles between two bowls and drizzle with the chilli oil.

Sprinkle with the spring onions and beni-shoga and serve.

yaki soba

serves 2

ingredients
400 g/14 oz ramen noodles
1 onion, finely sliced
200 g/7 oz beansprouts
1 red pepper, deseeded and
  sliced
150 g/5½ oz chicken,
  cooked and sliced
12 cooked peeled prawns
1 tbsp oil, for stir-frying
2 tbsp shoyu
½ tbsp mirin
1 tsp sesame oil
1 tsp sesame seeds
2 spring onions, finely sliced

> **>1** Cook the noodles according to the packet instructions, drain well, and tip into a bowl.

> **>2** Mix the onion, bean sprouts, red pepper, chicken and prawns together in a bowl. Stir through the noodles. Meanwhile, preheat a wok over high heat, add the oil and heat until very hot.

Sprinkle with sesame seeds
and spring onions and serve.

>3 Add the noodle mixture and stir-fry
for 4 minutes, or until golden, then add
the shoyu and sesame oil and toss
together.

>4 Divide the noodles between two bowls.

crab, asparagus & shiitake rolls with ponzu sauce

makes 24 pieces

ingredients

6 fresh asparagus spears
1 tbsp oil
6 shiitake mushrooms, sliced
1 quantity of sushi rice
  (see page 68)

6 small sheets toasted nori
wasabi paste
6 crab sticks, split in half
  lengthways

ponzu sauce
3 tbsp mirin
2 tbsp Japanese rice vinegar
1 tbsp usukuchi shoyu
  (Japanese light soy sauce)

2 tbsp bonito flakes
4 tbsp lemon juice

> **1** To make the sauce, put all the ingredients in a small pan and bring to the boil. Turn off the heat and let cool.

> **2** Fill a saucepan with water and simmer. Add the asparagus and cook until tender.

> **3** Cut the asparagus spears into 9-cm/3½-inch pieces and leave to cool.

> **4** Meanwhile, heat the oil in a frying pan and cook the mushrooms over medium heat for 5 minutes, or until completely soft.

> **5** Divide the rice into 6 equal portions. Put a sheet of nori, shiny-side down, on a sushi rolling mat with the longest end toward you. Using wet hands, spread 1 portion of the rice in an even layer on the nori, leaving 2 cm/¾ inch of nori visible at the end furthest away from you.

> **6** Spread a small amount of wasabi onto the rice at the end nearest to you. Top with an asparagus spear, then add 2 pieces of crab stick alongside. Add a line of mushroom slices.

> **7** Fold the mat over, starting at the end where the ingredients are and tucking in the end of the nori to start the roll. Keep rolling, lifting up the mat as you go and keeping the pressure even but gentle, until you have finished the roll. Moisten the top edge of the nori with water to seal the sushi roll closed.

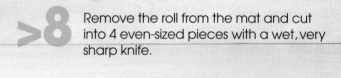

> **8** Remove the roll from the mat and cut into 4 even-sized pieces with a wet, very sharp knife.

Repeat with the remaining ingredients
and serve with the ponzu sauce.

sesame noodles with prawns

serves 2

ingredients

1 tbsp oil

16 raw prawns, peeled and deveined

3 shiitake mushrooms, finely sliced

¼ white or green cabbage, shredded

1 carrot, grated

2 bundles of somen noodles

6 shiso leaves, shredded

dressing

3 tbsp oil

1 tbsp sesame seeds, toasted

½ cup Japanese rice vinegar

1 tbsp sugar

1 tbsp usukuchi shoyu (Japanese light soy sauce)

salt, to taste

> **1** To make the dressing, mix 3 tablespoons of the oil and all the remaining ingredients together in a non metallic bowl.

> **2** Heat 1 tablespoon of the oil.

> **3** Add the prawns and cook until pink.

> **4** Add the mushrooms and stir-fry for 1 minute, then add the cabbage and carrot. Remove from the heat and leave to cool.

> 5 Cook the noodles according to the packet instructions, then drain.

> 6 Put the noodles in a bowl and add the prawn mixture, add the dressing and mix well.

Sprinkle with the shiso leaves and serve.

pho bo beef

serves 4

ingredients

2 litres/3½ pints rich beef stock
1 tbsp fresh ginger, finely sliced
1 garlic clove, thinly sliced
250 g/9 oz dried flat rice
  noodles
400 g/14 oz fillet or rump steak,
  thinly sliced into strips
4 spring onions, thinly sliced
125 g/4½ oz beansprouts
2 tbsp fish sauce
3 tbsp chopped coriander
chopped red chillies and soy
  sauce, to serve

>1 Heat the stock with the ginger and garlic until boiling, remove from the heat and leave to infuse for 10 minutes.

>2 Cook the rice noodles in boiling water for 3–4 minutes until just tender. Drain and divide between four deep bowls.

Serve the noodle soup immediately, with chillies and soy sauce to taste.

3 Top with the sliced beef and spring onions, then strain over the boiling stock.

4 Stir in the beansprouts, fish sauce and coriander.

fragrant rice with lemon grass & ginger

serves 4

ingredients

225 g/8 oz jasmine rice
25 g/1 oz butter
2.5-cm/1-inch piece fresh
   ginger, grated

250 ml/9 fl oz coconut milk
250 ml/9 fl oz water
½ tsp salt
½ tsp caster sugar
1 lemon grass stalk, bruised

2 dried kaffir lime leaves
curls of toasted fresh or dried
   coconut, to garnish

Soak the rice in cold water for 1 hour. Drain well.

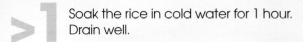

Melt the butter in a large pan and fry the rice on a high heat for 1 minute, stirring, until the grains are glossy.

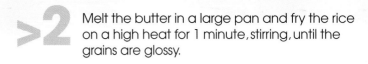

Add the ginger and cook, stirring, for 30 seconds, or until browned.

Stir in the coconut milk and water, then bring to the boil and add the salt and sugar.

>5 Reduce the heat and add the lemon grass and kaffir lime leaves. Cover and simmer gently for 10 minutes.

>6 Stir the rice, then place a tea towel over the pan, replace the lid and leave on a very low heat for 10 minutes.

Sprinkle with toasted coconut curls and serve as a side dish.

tea-smoked duck with jasmine rice

serves 4

ingredients

4 duck breasts, about 175 g/
6 oz each

2 tsp sea salt

1 tbsp Sichuan peppercorns,
without seeds, crushed

2 pieces star anise

55 g/2 oz black tea leaves

55 g/2 oz rice

1 tbsp dark muscovado sugar

300 g/10½ oz jasmine rice

2 tbsp coriander leaves,
chopped

4 spring onions, thinly sliced
diagonally

Score the skin of the duck breasts in a diamond pattern with a sharp knife.

Mix the salt and crushed peppercorns and rub into the duck breasts. Cover and leave to stand for 1 hour.

Grind together the star anise, tea, rice and sugar in a coffee grinder or processor. Line a wok with foil and scatter the mixture on the foil.

Place a wire rack over the foil and arrange the duck breasts on top, skin side down. Cover with a lid and tuck the foil around to seal.

>5 Place on a medium heat and when the tea begins to smoke, reduce the heat to low and leave for 10–12 minutes for rare, or 14–15 minutes for medium rare.

>6 Meanwhile, cook the jasmine rice in lightly salted boiling water for 10 minutes. Drain well and stir in the coriander.

Slice the duck and serve with the jasmine rice, scattered with sliced spring onions.

egg-fried rice
serves 4

ingredients
2 tbsp vegetable or groundnut
 oil
350 g/12 oz cooked rice, chilled
1 egg, well beaten

>1 Heat the oil in a preheated wok and stir-fry the rice for 1 minute.

>2 Using a fork, break down the rice as much as possible into individual grains.

Transfer the rice to bowls and serve.

>3 Quickly add the egg, stirring to coat each piece of rice.

>4 Continue to stir until the egg is cooked and the rice, as far as possible, is in single grains.

pad noodles with pork strips & prawns

serves 4

ingredients

250 g/9 oz flat rice noodles
200 g/7 oz pork fillet
3 tbsp groundnut oil
2 shallots, finely chopped

2 garlic cloves, finely chopped
175 g/6 oz raw prawns, peeled and deveined
2 eggs, beaten
2 tbsp Thai fish sauce

juice of 1 lime
1 tbsp tomato ketchup
2 tsp light muscovado sugar
½ tsp dried chilli flakes
100 g/3½ oz beansprouts

4 tbsp roasted salted peanuts, chopped
6 spring onions, diagonally sliced

> **1** Soak the noodles in hot water for 10 minutes, or according to the packet instructions. Drain well.

> **2** Slice the pork into strips about 5 mm/¼ inch thick.

> **3** Heat the oil in a wok and stir-fry the shallots for 1–2 minutes, to soften.

> **4** Add the pork strips and stir-fry for 2–3 minutes.

> 5 Add the garlic and prawns and stir-fry for 1–2 minutes.

> 6 Pour in the beaten eggs and stir for a few seconds until lightly set.

> 7 Reduce the heat and add the noodles, fish sauce, lime juice, ketchup and sugar. Toss together and heat through.

> 8 Sprinkle with chilli flakes, beansprouts, peanuts and spring onions.

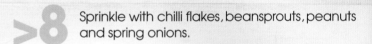

Transfer to bowls and serve.

ho fun noodles with beef strips

serves 4

ingredients

300 g/10½ oz rump or sirloin
  beef
2 tbsp soy sauce

2 tbsp sesame oil
250 g/9 oz flat rice noodles
2 tbsp groundnut oil
1 onion, sliced into thin wedges

2 garlic cloves, crushed
2.5-cm/1-inch piece fresh
  ginger, chopped
1 red chilli, thinly sliced

200 g/7 oz sprouting broccoli
½ Chinese cabbage, sliced
chilli oil, to serve

> **1** Slice the beef into thin strips, place in a bowl and sprinkle with soy sauce and sesame oil. Cover and leave to stand for 15 minutes.

> **2** Soak the noodles in hot water for 10 minutes or according to the packet instructions. Drain well.

> **3** Heat 1 tablespoon of groundnut oil in a wok and stir-fry the beef on a high heat until evenly coloured. Remove and keep to one side.

> **4** Add the remaining oil and stir-fry the onion, garlic, ginger and chilli for 1 minute.

>5 Add the broccoli and stir-fry for 2 minutes, then add the cabbage and stir-fry for 1 minute.

Add the beef with any marinade juices and stir until thoroughly heated, then spoon onto the noodles.

Serve immediately, drizzled with chilli oil.

chicken fried rice

serves 4

ingredients

½ tbsp sesame oil

6 shallots, peeled and cut into quarters

450 g/1 lb cooked chicken, cubed

3 tbsp soy sauce

2 carrots, diced

1 celery stick, diced

1 red pepper, deseeded and diced

175 g/6 oz fresh peas

100 g/3½ oz canned sweetcorn, drained

275 g/9¾ oz cooked long-grain rice

2 large eggs

>1 Heat the oil in a preheated wok or large frying pan over a medium heat.

>2 Add the shallots and fry until soft, then add the chicken and 2 tablespoons of the soy sauce and stir-fry for 5–6 minutes.

Transfer to bowls and serve immediately.

> **3** Stir in the carrots, celery, red pepper, peas and sweetcorn and stir-fry for a further 5 minutes.

> **4** Add the rice and stir thoroughly. Finally, beat the eggs and pour into the mixture. Stir until the eggs are beginning to set, then add in the remaining soy sauce.

egg noodles with tofu & mushrooms

serves 4

ingredients

3 tbsp groundnut oil
2 dried red chillies
250 g/9 oz medium egg
  noodles
1 garlic clove, crushed
200 g/7 oz firm tofu, cut into
  1-cm/½-inch cubes

200 g/7 oz oyster or chestnut
  mushrooms, sliced
2 tbsp lime juice
2 tbsp soy sauce
1 tsp brown sugar
fresh red chillies, to garnish

> 1
Heat the oil in a wok and add the chillies.
Heat gently for 10 minutes. Discard the
fried chillies.

> 2
Cook the noodles in boiling water for
4 minutes, or according to the packet
instructions. Drain.

> 3
Add the garlic and tofu to the wok
and stir-fry on a high heat until golden.
Remove with a slotted spoon and
keep hot.

> 4
Add the mushrooms to the wok and stir-fry for
2–3 minutes to soften.

>5 Stir in the lime juice, soy sauce and sugar.

>6 Return the noodles and tofu to the wok and toss to mix thoroughly.

Serve immediately, garnished with fresh chillies.

thai noodle salad

serves 4

ingredients

200 g/7 oz fine rice noodles
2 tbsp groundnut oil
1 red onion, thinly sliced
2 carrots, cut into matchsticks

125 g/4½ oz baby corn, halved
  lengthways
1 garlic clove, crushed
150 g/5½ oz beansprouts
2 tbsp fish sauce

juice of ½ lime
1 tsp caster sugar
½ tsp dried chilli flakes
4 tbsp coriander, chopped
4 spring onions, thinly sliced

40 g/1½ oz toasted peanuts
lime wedges, to serve

> 1 Soak the noodles in hot water for 10 minutes, or according to the packet instructions. Drain well.

> 2 Heat the oil in a wok and stir-fry the onion for 1 minute.

> 3 Add the carrots and corn and stir-fry for 2 minutes. Stir in the garlic then remove from the heat.

> 4 Stir in the beansprouts, then tip into a bowl and add the noodles, tossing to mix evenly.

Mix together the fish sauce, lime juice,
caster sugar, chillies and half the coriander.

>6
Spoon onto serving bowls, then
sprinkle with spring onions, peanuts
and the remaining coriander.

crispy noodles with pak choi in oyster sauce

serves 4

ingredients
groundnut oil, for deep-frying
100 g/3½ oz dried rice
    vermicelli noodles
1 tbsp crushed palm sugar or
    muscovado sugar
1 tbsp rice vinegar
1 tbsp fish sauce
1 tbsp lime juice
6 spring onions, sliced
1 garlic clove, thinly sliced
350 g/12 oz small pak choi,
    quartered lengthways
3 tbsp oyster sauce
sesame seeds, to sprinkle

1 Heat a deep pan of oil until a piece of noodle sizzles instantly. Add the noodles and fry in batches for 15–20 seconds, until puffed and golden. Drain on kitchen paper.

2 Heat the sugar, vinegar, fish sauce and lime juice in a small pan, until the sugar dissolves. Boil for 20–30 seconds until syrupy.

Serve the dish immediately,
sprinkled with sesame seeds.

>3 Heat 2 tablespoons of the oil in a wok
and stir-fry the spring onions and garlic for
1 minute. Add the pak choi and stir-fry
for 2–3 minutes. Stir in the oyster sauce.

>4 Toss the noodles with the syrup and serve with
the pak choi.

>1

>2

>3

main
meals

>4

>5

>6

gado gado

serves 4

ingredients

2 shallots, finely chopped
2 garlic cloves, crushed
3 tbsp groundnut oil
1 red chilli, finely chopped

juice of 2 limes
225 g/8 oz crunchy peanut
  butter
250 ml/9 fl oz coconut milk
200 g/7 oz French beans

½ cucumber
1 red pepper
250 g/9 oz tempeh or firm tofu,
  diced
200 g/7 oz beansprouts

2 heads Little Gem lettuce,
  chopped
2 hard-boiled eggs, quartered
chopped coriander, to garnish

Fry the shallots and garlic in 1 tablespoon of the oil for 2–3 minutes to soften but not brown.

Stir in the chilli, lime juice, peanut butter and coconut milk, and stir over a medium heat for 2–3 minutes. Cool.

> 3
Cut the beans into bite-sized pieces then blanch in boiling water for 2 minutes. Drain and rinse in cold water.

> 4
Halve the cucumber lengthways and slice diagonally. Deseed and thinly slice the red pepper.

> **5** Heat the remaining oil in a frying pan and fry the tempeh until golden on all sides. Drain on absorbent kitchen paper.

> **6** Toss together the beans, cucumber, red pepper, beansprouts and lettuce and arrange on a large platter.

> **7** Arrange the fried tempeh and hard-boiled eggs over the salad.

> **8** Spoon the dressing onto the salad and sprinkle with chopped coriander.

Serve immediately.

123

seafood curry

serves 4

ingredients

2 dried red chillies
2 tsp coriander seeds
1 tsp cumin seed
2 cardamom pods
1 tsp fenugreek seeds

1 tsp black peppercorns
1 tsp turmeric
1 tsp salt
500 g/1 lb 2 oz mixed fillets, e.g.
   tuna, haddock, mackerel
3 tbsp groundnut oil

1 large onion, chopped
2 garlic cloves, crushed
2.5-cm/1-inch piece fresh
   ginger, finely chopped
400 ml/14 fl oz canned
   coconut milk

400 g/14 oz canned chopped
   plum tomatoes
175 g/6 oz raw prawns, peeled
   and deveined
chopped fresh coriander,
   to garnish

>1 Place the chillies, coriander, cumin, cardamom, fenugreek and peppercorns in a heavy-based pan and stir on a high heat for 1 minute.

>2 Crush the spices finely with a pestle and mortar and add the turmeric and salt.

>3 Cut the fish into 5-cm/2-inch chunks and rub with half the spices. Cover and leave to one side.

>4 Heat half the oil in a large pan and fry the onion gently for 10 minutes, until soft and golden.

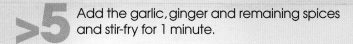

>5 Add the garlic, ginger and remaining spices and stir-fry for 1 minute.

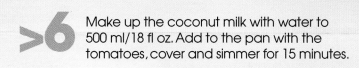

>6 Make up the coconut milk with water to 500 ml/18 fl oz. Add to the pan with the tomatoes, cover and simmer for 15 minutes.

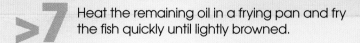

>7 Heat the remaining oil in a frying pan and fry the fish quickly until lightly browned.

>8 Add the fish and prawns to the sauce and simmer for 5-6 minutes.

Serve the curry immediately, garnished with chopped fresh coriander.

green chicken curry

serves 4

ingredients

2 tbsp groundnut or
  vegetable oil
4 spring onions, roughly
  chopped
2 tbsp green curry paste
700 ml/1¼ pints canned
  coconut milk
1 chicken stock cube
6 skinless chicken breasts, cut
  into 2.5-cm/1-inch cubes
large handful of fresh
  coriander, chopped
1 tsp salt
cooked rice, to serve

> **>1** Heat the oil in a preheated wok, add
> the spring onions and stir-fry over a
> medium–high heat for 30 seconds, or
> until starting to soften.

> **>2** Add the curry paste, coconut milk
> and stock cube and bring gently to
> the boil, stirring occasionally.

Serve immediately with rice.

>3 Add the chicken cubes, half the coriander and the salt and stir well. Reduce the heat and simmer gently for 8–10 minutes until the chicken is cooked through and tender.

>4 Stir in the remaining coriander.

teriyaki chicken

serves 4

ingredients

4 boneless chicken breasts, about 175 g/6 oz each, with or without skin

4 tbsp bottled teriyaki sauce
peanut or corn oil, for brushing

sesame noodles

250 g/9 oz dried thin buckwheat noodles
1 tbsp toasted sesame oil

2 tbsp sesame seeds, toasted
2 tbsp finely chopped fresh parsley
salt and pepper

>1 Using a sharp knife score each chicken breast diagonally across 3 times. Rub all over with teriyaki sauce. Set aside in the refrigerator to marinate for at least 10 minutes and up to 24 hours.

>2 Preheat the grill to high. Bring a saucepan of water to the boil, add the buckwheat noodles and cook according to the packet instructions. Drain and rinse well in cold water.

>3 Lightly brush the griddle pan with oil. Add the chicken breasts, skin side up, and brush again with a little extra teriyaki sauce.

>4 Griddle the chicken breast, brushing occasionally with extra teriyaki sauce, for 15 minutes, or until cooked through and the juices run clear when pierced with a skewer.

Meanwhile, heat a wok over high heat. Add the sesame oil and heat until it shimmers.

Add the noodles and stir round to heat through, then stir in the sesame seeds and parsley. Add salt and pepper to taste.

Transfer the chicken breasts to plates and add a portion of noodles to each.

chicken with cashew nuts

serves 4–6

ingredients

450 g/1 lb boneless chicken meat, cut into bite-sized pieces
3 tbsp light soy sauce
1 tsp Shaoxing rice wine

pinch of sugar
½ tsp salt
3 dried Chinese mushrooms, soaked in warm water for 20 minutes

2 tbsp vegetable or groundnut oil
4 slices of fresh ginger
1 tsp finely chopped garlic

1 red pepper, deseeded and cut into 2.5-cm/1-inch squares
85 g/3 oz cashew nuts, toasted

134

> **1** Marinate the chicken in 2 tablespoons of the light soy sauce, Shaoxing, sugar and salt for at least 20 minutes.

> **2** Squeeze any excess water from the mushrooms and finely slice, discarding any tough stems. Reserve the soaking water.

> **3** In a preheated wok, heat 1 tablespoon of the oil. Add the ginger and stir-fry until fragrant. Stir in the chicken and cook for 2 minutes, until it turns brown. Before the chicken is cooked through, remove and set aside.

> **4** Clean the wok, heat the remaining oil and stir-fry the garlic until fragrant. Add the mushrooms and red pepper and stir-fry for 1 minute.

>5 Add about 2 tablespoons of the mushroom soaking water and cook for about 2 minutes until the water has evaporated.

>6 Return the chicken to the wok, add the remaining light soy sauce and the cashew nuts and stir-fry for 2 minutes until the chicken is cooked through.

Transfer to bowls and serve.

> **1** To prepare the duck, massage the skin to separate it from the meat. Pour the boiling water into a large pan, add the honey, Shaoxing and vinegar and lower in the duck. Baste for about 1 minute. Remove the duck and hang it to dry for 2 hours, or overnight.

> **2** Preheat the oven to 200°C/400°F/ Gas Mark 6. Place the duck on a rack above a roasting tin and roast for at least 1 hour until the skin is very crispy and the duck cooked through.

Roll up and eat. Repeat the process with the lean meat.

> **>3** Shred the white parts of the spring onions. Place the duck on a chopping board, together with the cucumber, spring onions and pancakes, and carve off the skin first.

> **>4** On a pancake, arrange a little skin with some cucumber and spring onion. Top with a little plum sauce.

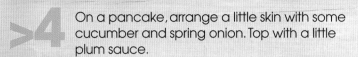

ginger pork with shiitake mushrooms

serves 4

ingredients

2 tbsp vegetable oil
3 shallots, finely chopped
2 garlic cloves, crushed
5-cm/2-inch piece fresh ginger, thinly sliced

500 g/1 lb 2 oz pork stir-fry strips
250 g/9 oz shiitake mushrooms, sliced
4 tbsp soy sauce
4 tbsp rice wine
1 tsp light muscovado sugar

1 tsp cornflour
2 tbsp cold water
3 tbsp chopped fresh coriander, to garnish

> 1 Heat the oil in a wok and fry the shallots for 2–3 minutes, to soften.

> 2 Add the garlic and ginger and stir-fry for 1 minute.

> 3 Add the pork strips and stir-fry for 1 minute.

> 4 Add the mushrooms and stir-fry for a further 2–3 minutes.

141

>5 Stir in the soy sauce, rice wine and sugar.

>6 Blend the cornflour and water until smooth, add to the pan, stirring, and cook until the juices are thickened and clear.

Serve the stir-fry garnished with coriander.

fried tofu with lemon grass

serves 6

ingredients

3 tbsp fish sauce
3 tbsp freshly squeezed lime or
  lemon juice
3 tbsp palm sugar or
  granulated sugar

1 lemon grass stalk
vegetable oil, for frying
1 large shallot, finely chopped
1 large garlic clove, finely
  chopped

1 red bird's eye chilli, deseeded
  and finely chopped
900 g/2 lb firm or extra-firm tofu,
  drained and cut crossways
  into 1 cm/½ inch thick
  rectangular slices

6 sprigs fresh coriander,
  trimmed, to garnish

> **1** Put the fish sauce, lime juice and sugar in a non-reactive bowl and whisk until the sugar is completely dissolved. Reserve.

> **2** Discard the bruised leaves and root end of the lemon grass stalk, then finely grate 15–20 cm/6–8 inches of the lower stalk.

> **3** Heat 2 tablespoons of oil in a small saucepan over a high heat, then add the lemon grass, shallot, garlic and chilli and stir-fry for 5 minutes, or until fragrant and golden.

> **4** Transfer to the fish sauce mixture and stir well. Reserve.

> **5** Working in batches if necessary, heat 2 tablespoons of oil in a non-stick frying pan, then add the tofu slices and fry over a high heat, turning often, for 6 minutes, or until golden and crisp on both sides.

> **6** Drain on a plate lined with kitchen paper. If cooking in batches, add extra oil to the frying pan as needed. Transfer to plates and serve.

Transfer the fried tofu to a serving platter and spoon the herb sauce over each slice, then garnish with the coriander sprigs.

beef chop suey

serves 4

ingredients

450 g/1 lb ribeye steak, sliced
1 head broccoli, cut into florets
2 tbsp vegetable oil
1 onion, sliced
2 sticks celery, sliced
225 g/8 oz mangetout, sliced lengthways
55 g/2 oz canned bamboo shoots, rinsed
    and shredded
8 water chestnuts, sliced
225 g/8 oz mushrooms, sliced
1 tbsp oyster sauce
1 tsp salt

marinade

1 tbsp Shaoxing rice wine
½ tsp white pepper
½ tsp salt
1 tbsp light soy sauce
½ tsp sesame oil

> 1 Combine all the marinade ingredients in a bowl, and marinate the beef for at least 20 minutes.

> 2 Blanch the broccoli in a large pan of boiling water for 30 seconds. Drain and set aside.

Transfer to bowls and serve.

>3 In a preheated wok, heat 1 tablespoon of the oil and stir-fry the beef until the colour has changed. Remove and set aside.

>4 Clean the wok, heat the remaining oil and stir-fry the onion for 1 minute. Add the celery and broccoli and cook for 2 minutes. Add the mangetout, bamboo shoots, water chestnuts and mushrooms and cook for 1 minute. Add the beef and season with the oyster sauce and salt.

sichuan noodles

serves 4

ingredients

250 g/9 oz thick egg noodles
2 tbsp peanut or corn oil
2 large garlic cloves, very finely
    chopped

1 large red onion, cut in half
    and thinly sliced
125 ml/4 fl oz vegetable stock
    or water
2 tbsp bottled chilli bean sauce

2 tbsp Chinese sesame paste
1 tbsp dried Sichuan
    peppercorns, roasted and
    ground
1 tsp light soy sauce

2 small bok choi or other
    Chinese cabbage, cut into
    quarters
1 large carrot, grated

150

> **1** Cook the noodles in a saucepan of boiling water for 4 minutes, until soft.

> **2** Drain and rinse with cold water and set aside.

> **3** Heat a wok over high heat and add the oil.

> **4** Add the garlic and onion and stir-fry for 1 minute.

> **5** Add the vegetable stock, chilli bean sauce, sesame paste, ground Sichuan peppercorns and soy sauce and bring to the boil, stirring to blend the ingredients together.

> **6** Add the bok choi quarters and grated carrot and continue to stir-fry for 1–2 minutes, until they are just wilted.

> **7** Add the noodles and continue stir-frying,

> **8** Using 2 forks, mix all the ingredients together until the noodles are hot.

Transfer to bowls and serve.

red-cooked duck with bamboo shoots

serves 4

ingredients

2.5 kg/5 lb 8 oz oven ready
  duck with giblets
3 shallots, chopped
2 garlic cloves, sliced

2.5-cm/1-inch piece fresh
  ginger, sliced
2 tsp Chinese five spice paste
2 pieces star anise
100 ml/3½ fl oz rice wine

3 tbsp soy sauce
2 tbsp brown sugar
1 litre/1¾ pints water, approx
1 tsp cornflour
4 tbsp plum sauce

225 g/8 oz canned bamboo
  shoots, drained and cut into
  matchsticks
chopped coriander, to garnish
boiled rice, to serve

> 1 Place the duck in a large pan, breast side down. Add the shallots, garlic, ginger, spice paste, anise, rice wine, soy sauce and sugar.

> 2 Pour over just enough water to cover the duck. Bring to the boil, cover and simmer for 1 hour, turning once.

> 3 Lift out the duck and discard the giblets. Cut the duck into 8 pieces, discarding the backbone.

> 4 Strain the liquid, skim off the fat, and boil to reduce to about 500 ml/18 fl oz.

> **5** Mix the cornflour with 1 tbsp cold water, stir into the sauce and cook until thickened. Add the plum sauce.

> **6** Add the duck pieces to the sauce and simmer for 8–10 minutes, turning occasionally. Add the bamboo shoots.

Serve the duck with boiled rice, sprinkled
with coriander.

sliced beef in black bean sauce

serves 4

ingredients
3 tbsp groundnut oil
450 g/1 lb beef sirloin, thinly sliced
1 red pepper, deseeded and thinly sliced
1 green pepper, deseeded and thinly sliced
1 bunch spring onions, sliced
2 garlic cloves, crushed
1 tbsp grated fresh ginger
2 tbsp black bean sauce
1 tbsp sherry
1 tbsp soy sauce

> **>1** Heat 2 tbsp oil in a wok and stir-fry the beef on a high heat for 1–2 minutes. Remove and keep to one side.

> **>2** Add the remaining oil and peppers and stir-fry for 2 minutes.

Transfer to bowls and serve.

>3 Add the spring onions, garlic and ginger and stir-fry for 30 seconds.

>4 Add the black bean sauce, sherry and soy sauce, then stir in the beef and heat until bubbling.

159

honey-glazed roast pork

serves 4

ingredients

2 tbsp clear honey
1 tbsp rice vinegar
2 tbsp light brown sugar
1 tbsp hoisin sauce

1 tbsp light soy sauce
2 tsp five spice paste
500 g/1 lb 2 oz pork fillet, in one piece
3 tbsp rice wine

1 tsp cornflour
175 ml/6 fl oz chicken stock
stir-fried vegetables, to serve

> **1** Mix together the honey, vinegar, sugar, hoisin sauce, soy sauce and peppercorns in a wide, non-metallic bowl and spice paste. Pour over the pork. Cover and leave to marinate in the fridge overnight.

> **2** Preheat the oven to 200°C/400°F/Gas Mark 6. Drain the pork, reserving the marinade, and place on a wire rack in a roasting tin.

> **3** Pour a 2.5-cm/1-inch depth of boiling water into the tin and place in the oven for 20 minutes.

> **4** Turn the pork over, brush with the marinade, then cook for a further 20 minutes, or until there is no trace of pink in the juices.

Mix the rice wine and cornflour to a
smooth paste, then place in a pan with the
reserved marinade and stock.

Bring to boiling point, whilst stirring,
then simmer for 2 minutes until
thickened and clear.

Slice the pork thinly and serve with the sauce spooned over. Serve with stir-fried vegetables.

thai fish cakes

serves 4

ingredients
1 garlic clove, sliced
1 shallot, finely chopped
1 lemon grass stalk, finely
   chopped
2.5-cm/1-inch piece galangal,
   finely chopped

4 tbsp coriander, chopped
1 tbsp fish sauce
1 small egg, beaten
50 g/1 lb 2 oz skinless white
   fish fillets
groundnut oil, for frying

sauce
5-cm/2-inch piece cucumber
1 small red chilli
1 tsp palm sugar or muscovado
   sugar
juice of 1 lime
2 tbsp light soy sauce

> 1 Place the garlic, shallot, lemon grass, galangal, coriander, fish sauce and egg in a food processor and process until smooth.

> 2 Cut the fish into chunks, add to the processor and process in short bursts until very finely chopped.

> 3 Divide the mixture into 12–16 pieces, roll into balls with your hands, then flatten to patty shapes.

> 4 To make the sauce, cut the cucumber into fine dice and finely chop the chilli.

> **5** Mix together the sugar, lime juice and soy sauce, stirring until the sugar dissolves. Add the cucumber and chilli.

> **6** Heat a shallow depth of oil in a frying pan and fry the fish cakes in batches until golden, turning once.

Lift out the fish cakes and drain on absorbent kitchen paper.

Transfer the fish cakes to kitchen paper.

Serve the fish cakes hot, with the chilli sauce for dipping.

sichuan peppered beef

serves 4

ingredients
2.5-cm/1-inch piece fresh
  ginger, grated
1 garlic clove, crushed
1 tbsp rice wine
1 tbsp soy sauce
1 tbsp hoisin sauce
2 tsp Sichuan peppercorns,
  without seeds, crushed
600 g/1 lb 5 oz beef fillet
3 tbsp groundnut oil
1 onion, thinly sliced
1 green pepper, deseeded
  and thinly sliced

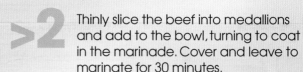

>1 Mix together the ginger, garlic, rice wine,
soy sauce, hoisin sauce and peppercorns in
a wide, non-metallic bowl.

>2 Thinly slice the beef into medallions
and add to the bowl, turning to coat
in the marinade. Cover and leave to
marinate for 30 minutes.

Serve the beef immediately.

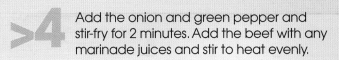

>3 Heat the oil in a wok and stir-fry the beef for 1–2 minutes to brown. Remove and keep to one side.

>4 Add the onion and green pepper and stir-fry for 2 minutes. Add the beef with any marinade juices and stir to heat evenly.

>1

>2

>3

desserts

>4

>5

>6

coconut pancakes with pineapple

serves 4

ingredients
140 g/5 oz plain flour
2 tbsp caster sugar
2 eggs

400 ml/14 fl oz coconut milk
1 medium pineapple
groundnut oil, for frying
toasted coconut, to decorate

canned coconut cream,
  to serve

> **1** Sift the flour and sugar into a bowl and make a well in the centre.

> **2** Add the eggs and coconut milk to the well and stir into the flour, then whisk to a smooth, bubbly batter.

> **3** Cut off the skin of the pineapple, remove the core and cut the flesh into chunks.

> **4** Heat a small amount of oil in a heavy-based frying pan and pour in a little batter, swirling to cover the pan.

Cook the pancake on a high heat until set and golden underneath.

 Toss or turn the pancake and cook until golden on the other side.

>7 Repeat with the remaining batter to make 8–10 pancakes, stacking alternately with non-stick paper between whilst making the rest.

>8 Fill the pancakes with pieces of pineapple and fold into fan shapes to serve.

Sprinkle the pancakes with toasted shreds of coconut and serve drizzled with coconut cream.

green tea ice cream

serves 4

ingredients
225 ml/8 fl oz milk
2 egg yolks

2 tbsp caster sugar
2 tbsp green tea powder
90 ml/3 fl oz hot water

225 ml/8 fl oz double cream,
   lightly whipped

> **1** Pour the milk into a pan and heat to boiling point. Meanwhile, whisk the egg yolks with the sugar in a heatproof bowl.

> **2** Pour the milk onto the egg mixture, stirring constantly, then pour all the mixture back into the pan and stir well.

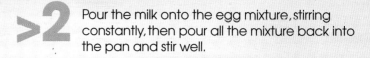

> **3** Cook over low heat, stirring constantly, for 3 minutes, or until the mixture is thick enough to coat the back of a spoon. Remove from the heat and let cool.

> **4** Mix the green tea powder with the hot water in a jug, pour into the cooled custard and mix well.

>5 Fold in the cream. Transfer to a freezerproof container and freeze for 2 hours.

>6 Turn into a bowl and beat with a fork to break down the ice crystals, then return to the freezerproof container and freeze for an additional 2 hours. Beat again, then return to the freezer and freeze overnight, or until solid.

Transfer to bowls and serve.

coconut ice cream

serves 4

ingredients
400 ml/14 fl oz coconut milk
140 g/5 oz caster sugar
150 m/5 fl oz single cream
rind of ½ lime, finely grated
2 tbsp lime juice
curls of lime zest to decorate

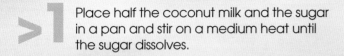

>1 Place half the coconut milk and the sugar in a pan and stir on a medium heat until the sugar dissolves.

>2 Remove from the heat and stir in the remaining coconut milk, cream, lime rind and juice. Leave to cool completely.

Top with curled shreds of lime
zest and serve.

 3 Transfer to a freezerproof container
and freeze for 2 hours, whisking at
hourly intervals.

 4 Serve the ice cream scooped into glasses or
bowls.

almond tea jelly

serves 4–6

ingredients

410 g can evaporated milk
40 g/1½ oz ground rice
40 g/1½ oz caster sugar

55 g/2 oz ground almonds
1 tsp almond extract
1 sachet of gelatine
4 tbsp hot water

2 tsp jasmine blossom tea
 leaves
rose petals, to decorate

Place the evaporated milk and ground rice in a pan and heat, stirring, until boiling.

Remove from the heat and stir in the sugar, almonds and almond extract. Cover and leave to stand for 10 minutes.

Dissolve the gelatine in a bowl of water placed over a pan of hot water.

Stir the gelatine mixture into the milk mixture.

>7 Strain the tea, then leave to cool and chill in the refrigerator.

>8 Cut the almond jelly into diamond shapes and arrange in wide individual bowls.

Spoon the tea around the jellies and
scatter with rose petals to serve.

spiced mung bean pots

serves 6

ingredients

85 g/3 oz mung beans
100 g/3½ oz caster sugar

2 tbsp rice flour
½ tsp ground cinnamon
½ tsp ground ginger

finely grated rind 1 lime
1 large egg
125 ml/4 fl oz coconut milk

whipped cream and freshly
grated nutmeg, to serve

> 1 Place the beans in a pan and cover with boiling water. Bring to the boil, cover and simmer for about 30 minutes or until tender.

> 2 Drain the beans well and press through a sieve to make a smooth purée.

> 3 Sift the sugar, flour and spices into a bowl and add the bean purée and lime rind.

> 4 Beat the egg with the coconut milk and stir into the bowl, mixing evenly.

>5 Place a steamer on to heat. Spoon the mixture into six 100-ml/3½-fl oz heatproof dishes.

>6 Cover the dishes tightly with foil and place in the steamer.

>7 Steam for 20–25 minutes or until lightly set. Remove the foil and cool slightly.

>8 To serve, top with a spoonful of whipped cream and sprinkle with nutmeg.

Serve immediately.

lychee sherbert

serves 4

ingredients

400 g/14 oz canned lychees,
   or 450 g/1 lb fresh lychees,
   peeled and pitted

2 tbsp icing sugar
1 egg white
1 lemon, thinly sliced,
   to decorate

>**1** Put the lychee flesh into a blender or food processor with the sugar. Blend to a purée.

>**2** Press the lychee purée through a strainer to remove any remaining solid pieces,

Decorate with lemon slices and serve.

>3 Transfer to a freezerproof container, and freeze for 3 hours.

>4 Turn the mixture into the blender or food processor and blend until slushy. Keeping the motor running, add the egg white, then return the mixture to the freezerproof container and freeze for 8 hours or overnight.

fried banana dumplings

serves 6

ingredients

vegetable oil, for deep-frying
140 g/5 oz plain flour
2 tbsp granulated sugar or
  palm sugarr

½ tsp salt
2 tsp baking powder
2 large eggs
350 ml/12 fl oz canned
  coconut milk

12 small, ripe Asian bananas,
  peeled
icing sugar, for dusting

>1 Half-fill a small to medium saucepan with oil and heat over a medium-high heat to 180–190°C/350–375°F, or until a cube of bread browns in 30 seconds.

>2 Meanwhile, put the flour, granulated sugar, salt and baking powder in a medium–large bowl.

>3 Whisk to combine the ingredients. Make a well in the centre and add the eggs and coconut milk.

>4 Whisk, gradually incorporating the dry ingredients into the wet ingredients, until the batter is smooth. Add the bananas to the batter, making sure they are coated evenly all over.

>5 Working in batches, lower the bananas into the hot oil and deep-fry for 5–7 minutes, or until golden and crisp.

>6 Drain the bananas on a plate lined with kitchen paper.

Transfer to plates and serve, dusted with
icing sugar.

almond biscuits

makes about 50 pieces

ingredients

675 g/1 lb 8 oz plain flour
½ tsp baking powder
½ tsp salt

100 g/3½ oz slivered almonds
225 g/8 oz lard, cut into tiny
   cubes
225 g/8 oz white sugar

1 egg, lightly beaten
1½ tsp almond essence
50 whole almonds, to decorate
   (optional)

> 1
Preheat the oven to 160°C/325°F/Gas Mark 3. Sift the flour, baking powder and salt together and set aside.

> 2
Pulverize the almond slivers in a food processor, add the flour mixture and pulse until the nuts are well mixed with the flour.

> 3
Turn the flour and nut mixture into a large bowl, add the lard and work into the flour until crumbly.

> 4
Add the sugar, egg and almond essence and mix well until the dough is soft and pliable but still firm enough to be handled.

Divide the dough into 2.5-cm/1-inch balls. Place on a lined baking trays 5-cm/2-inches apart, and flatten with the back of a spoon.

Press a whole almond (if using) onto each biscuit. Bake for 15–18 minutes.

Transfer to a wire rack to cool and serve.

mango with sticky rice squares

serves 4

ingredients
200 g/7 oz jasmine rice
250 ml/9 fl oz canned
  coconut milk
250 ml/9 fl oz water
85 g/3 oz caster sugar
2 ripe mangoes
juice of 1 lime
shreds of lime zest, to decorate

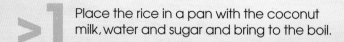 **>1** Place the rice in a pan with the coconut milk, water and sugar and bring to the boil.

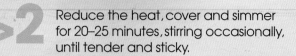 **>2** Reduce the heat, cover and simmer for 20–25 minutes, stirring occasionally, until tender and sticky.

Serve the rice squares with slices of mango, drizzled with purée and sprinkled with shreds of lime.

>3 Spread the rice in a greased 20-cm/ 8-inch square tin and leave to set. Cut into 4 squares when set.

>4 Peel, stone and slice the mangoes and sprinkle with lime juice. Reserve a few slices and purée the rest in a food processor.

malaysian milk pudding

serves 4

ingredients

40 g/1½ oz vermicelli rice
  noodles
40 g/1½ oz butter

700 ml/1¼ pints milk
125 ml/4 fl oz coconut cream
30 g/1 oz caster sugar
1 cinnamon stick

3 cardamom pods
40 g/1½ oz sultanas
½ tsp almond extract

pinch of ground turmeric
2 tbsp flaked almonds

>1 Break the noodles into 5-cm/2-inch lengths.

>2 Heat 30 g/1 oz butter in a large pan and fry the noodles, stirring, until pale golden.

>3 Add the milk, coconut cream, sugar, cinnamon and cardamom and stir until almost boiling.

>4 Reduce the heat, cover and simmer for 10–12 minutes, stirring occasionally.

Add the sultanas, almond extract and turmeric and simmer for 5 minutes. Cool.

Fry the almonds in the remaining butter until golden.

Transfer to bowls, sprinkle with almonds and serve.

oriental fruit salad

serves 4-6

ingredients
1 lime
2 lemon grass stalks, bruised
55 g/2 oz caster sugar
100 ml/3½ fl oz boiling water

400 g/14 oz slice watermelon
half a Galia melon, about
  350 g/12 oz in weight
1 dragon fruit
1 starfruit

sprigs of mint, to decorate
coconut ice cream, to serve
  (optional)

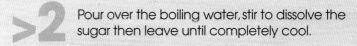

>1 Pare a thin strip of rind from the lime and place in a heatproof jug with the lemon grass and sugar.

>2 Pour over the boiling water, stir to dissolve the sugar then leave until completely cool.

>3 Peel and deseed the melons and chop these and the dragon fruit into bite-sized chunks.

>4 Trim the starfruit and cut into thin slices.

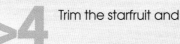

>5 Combine all the fruits in a wide bowl and squeeze over the juice of the lime.

>6 Strain the lemon grass syrup, pour over the fruit and stir lightly.

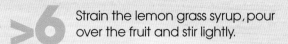

Transfer to bowls, sprinkle with mint and serve with ice cream, if using.

baked passion fruit custards

serves 4

ingredients
4 passion fruit
4 large eggs
175 ml/6 fl oz coconut milk
55 g/2 oz caster sugar
1 tsp orange flower water

>1 Preheat the oven to 180°C/350°F/Gas Mark 4. Halve 3 passion fruit, scoop out the flesh and rub through a sieve to remove the seeds.

>2 Beat together the eggs, passion fruit juice, coconut milk, sugar and orange flower water until smooth.

Serve the custards slightly warm, or chilled.

>3 Pour the custard into four 200-ml/7-fl oz ovenproof dishes, place in a baking tin and pour in hot water to reach halfway up the dishes.

>4 Bake in the oven for 40–45 minutes or until just set. Scoop the pulp from the remaining passion fruit and spoon a little onto each dish to serve.

toffee sweet potatoes

serves 4

ingredients

450 g/1 lb sweet potatoes,
  scrubbed
groundnut oil, for frying

140 g/5 oz sugar
1 tsp soy sauce
75 ml/2½ fl oz water
2 tsp sesame seeds

>1 Cut the potatoes into 1 cm/½ inch thick slices, leaving the peel on.

>2 Cut each slice crossways to make four wedges.

>3 Heat a 2.5-cm/1-inch depth of oil in a wok to 180–190°C/350–375°F, or until a cube of bread browns in 30 seconds. Fry the potatoes in batches for 2–3 minutes until golden.

>4 Remove with a slotted spoon and drain on absorbent kitchen paper.

Place the sugar, soy sauce and water in a pan and stir on a low heat until the sugar dissolves.

Boil the mixture until it becomes syrupy and darkens to a rich toffee colour. Remove from the heat.

Quickly toss the pieces of potato in the toffee, turning to coat evenly.

Lift onto non-stick paper and sprinkle with sesame seeds. Leave to cool.

Serve the toffee potatoes immediately.

burmese semolina cake

serves 4

ingredients

115 g/4 oz butter
250 g/9 oz coarse semolina
400 ml/14 fl oz canned
  coconut milk

400 ml/14 fl oz water
140 g/5 oz light muscovado
  sugar
½ tsp ground cardamom
4 eggs, beaten

55 g/2 oz sultanas
2 tbsp white poppy seeds or
  sesame seeds

> **1** Preheat the oven to 200°C/400°F/Gas Mark 6. Grease a 23-cm/9-inch square cake tin with 1 tablespoon of butter.

> **2** Place the semolina in a heavy-based pan and toast on a fairly high heat, stirring until pale golden.

> **3** Stir in the coconut milk, water and sugar then simmer, stirring constantly, until thickened.

> **4** Remove from the heat and beat in the remaining butter, cardamom, eggs and sultanas.

> **5** Spread the mixture into the tin and sprinkle with poppy seeds.

> **6** Bake for 40–45 minutes, until firm and golden. Cool in the tin, then cut into squares or diamond shapes.

Serve the cake cold as a sweetmeat, or warm with fresh fruit for dessert.

sweet wontons

serves 4

ingredients
85 g/3 oz dates, stoned
1 banana
55 g/2 oz blanched almonds
½ tsp ground cinnamon
20 wonton wrappers
1 egg white, lightly beaten
groundnut oil, for deep-frying
icing sugar, for dusting

>1 Peel the banana. Roughly chop the dates, banana and almonds, then mix with the cinnamon.

>2 Place 1 teaspoon of the fruit mixture in the centre of each wonton wrapper.

Serve the wontons hot, lightly
dusted with icing sugar.

>3 Brush the edges of the wonton with
egg white, pull up the sides then pinch
together to seal. Pull out the corners.

>4 Heat enough oil for deep-frying in a wok
or large pan to 180-190°C/350-370°F or until
a cube of bread browns in 30 seconds.
Deep-fry the wontons for 1–2 minutes,
turning occasionally, until golden. Drain
on kitchen paper.

Index